To

with sisterly love

From

Sisters

Words from the Heart

new seasons™

New Seasons is a trademark of Publications International, Ltd.

Louis Weber, CEO
Publications International, Ltd.
7373 North Cicero Avenue
Lincolnwood, Illinois 60712

Manufactured in China.

8 7 6 5 4 3 2 1

0-7853-2287-6

n e w   s e a s o n s™
a division of Publications International, Ltd.

ONTENTS

GIRLS TOGETHER

GIRLS
TOGETHER

*G*rowing up, sisters weave
a unique bond that ties them
to each other with silken
skeins of love, laughter, and
memories.

As children, the dedicated softball player and the devoted ballet student busily headed in different directions. As adults, the athlete admires her sister's easy grace and unflappable poise. The dancer cherishes her sister's matter-of-fact willingness to step up to bat no matter what the situation.

GIRLS TOGETHER

SISTERS

GIRLS TOGETHER

THE CHILDREN'S HOUR

...From my study, I see in the
lamplight,
Descending the broad hall stair,
Grave Alice and laughing Allegra
and Edith with golden hair...

They climb up into my turret
oer' the arms and back of my chair;
If I try to escape they surround me;
They seem to be everywhere.

❧

GIRLS TOGETHER

SISTERS

...I have you fast in my fortress
And will not let you depart,
But put you down into the dungeon
In the round-tower of my heart...

And there will I keep you forever.

HENRY WADSWORTH LONGFELLOW
1807–1882

GIRLS TOGETHER

GIRLS TOGETHER

*O*nce a big sister always a big sister, and little sisters won't be big sisters no matter how much they grow. This reality, so distressing when you're 6 or 7, can be infinitely comforting at 29 or 30.

GIRLS TOGETHER

There's a special kind of freedom sisters enjoy. Freedom to share innermost thoughts, to ask a favor, to show their true feelings. The freedom to simply be themselves.

ANONYMOUS

GIRLS TOGETHER

*O*nly a sister protests
when you want to wear
her new hat first and then
grudgingly tells you it
looks best on you.

Girls Together

15

GIRLS TOGETHER

When you and your sister used the good dishes to play house, climbed the backyard tree and couldn't get down, cut each other's hair to practice for a possible future as a beautician, and brewed mud tea on the kitchen table, you blamed your sister for getting you into trouble. It's only fair that now you thank her for all those glorious memories.

❧

A sister carries precious bits of people she loves carefully stored in her memory. How comforting when you're troubled to have your sister offer some of Mother's warmth mixed with measures of Dad's common sense and Grandpa's humor.

GIRLS TOGETHER

GIRLS TOGETHER

What strong,
mysterious links enchain
the heart to regions
where the morn of life
was spent.

JAMES GRAHAME
1765–1811

GIRLS TOGETHER

HEART TO HEART

22

HEART
TO HEART

A special love flows
between sisters, as joyful as a
bubbling brook, as deep as a
mighty river, and as
indomitable as a swift
mountain stream.

HEART TO HEART

A sister is a gift of
God, sent from above to
make life worthwhile
here below.

ANONYMOUS

The years weave a bond of love among sisters. At first glance, this seems to be an uncomplicated connection, but examine it closely and you'll discover threads of memory entwined with trust, hope, laughter, and tears.

HEART TO HEART

HEART TO HEART

28

The whole room seems to
brighten when your sister smiles.
No wonder. The light of your shared
lives shines in her face—the glimmer
of childhood innocence, the blaze
of teenage energy, the radiance
of full-speed-ahead adulthood
as well as the mellow glow of
countless good times to come.

A sister remembers times when you were almost perfect and times when you were anything but, and she loves you all the more for both.

HEART TO HEART

HEART TO HEART

*S*isters count on
each other's strengths and
compensate for each
other's weaknesses.

*I*n childhood, you and your sisters start a relationship that becomes like Grandmother's fine china. When you take it out after years of storage and dust it gently, you'll discover that it's even more beautiful than you remember. And its value has increased immeasurably over the years.

SISTERS

HEART TO HEART

The only child believes that she isn't missing anything by not having sisters. It's just as well that she never will know better.

HEART TO HEART

HAND IN HAND

HAND
IN HAND

*S*isters count on each
other—unfailing support,
honest advice, little favors,
impossible impositions, and
whatever else is required.

HAND IN HAND

Oh, the comfort, the inexpressible
comfort, of feeling safe with a person,
having neither to weigh thoughts nor
measure words, but pouring them all
right out, just as they are, chaff and grain
together; certain that a faithful hand will
take and sift them, keep what is worth
keeping and then with the breath of
kindness throw the rest away.

DINAH MARIA MULOCK CRAIK
1826–1887

HAND IN HAND

A good sister will respond politely to an invitation, but she won't wait for one if she thinks you need her.

HAND IN HAND

*S*ometimes when you try to engage your sister in a serious discussion, the most positive thing she can do is help you see that the situation isn't so serious after all.

HAND IN HAND

HAND IN HAND

When the world weighs heavy on your shoulders, count on your sister to remind you that no one asked you to pick it up in the first place.

When you've made a mistake that you need to get off your chest, tell your sister. She won't be surprised; she's seen you through all sorts of jams. She probably won't be worried either; she's also seen you solve all kinds of problems. To top it off, she probably did something similar that she'll share with you. With your sister's reassurance, the problem dwindles.

HAND IN HAND

HAND IN HAND

Tell someone else
your problems and you
may receive sympathy.
From a sister, you can
depend on empathy.

One sister bakes the cake, the second comes up with clever decorations for the party, and the third writes gracious thank-you notes to everyone who came. After so many years together, the trio has learned to appreciate and depend on each other's talents.

HAND IN HAND

HAND IN HAND

A sister gives priceless advice. Even though she knows what you want her to say, she will tell you what she thinks you need to hear.

FOREVER FRIENDS

FOREVER
FRIENDS

Better than best, longer than longest, and enduring beyond all others, friendship between sisters reaches heights other relationships cannot touch.

For there is no friend
like a sister
In calm or stormy weather;
To cheer one on the
tedious way,
To fetch one if one goes astray,
To lift one if one totters down,
To strengthen whilst one
stands.

CHRISTINA ROSSETTI
1830–1894

FOREVER FRIENDS

*M*uch of a garden's beauty is
in its diversity. One sister is as bouncy
and bold as a black-eyed Susan; another
as shy and delicate as a pale-pink lady's
slipper. The third is showy and passionate
like a deep purple iris, with humor and
optimism that only could be termed

perennial. The fourth sister is Queen Anne's lace, so purely pretty that you'd never guess she also is dependable and hardy. Each shines with a loveliness all her own, and no one would wish one's characteristics for the other.

FOREVER FRIENDS

A true sister is a friend who listens with her heart.

ANONYMOUS

*S*isters can be so
different from the friends they
choose: serious and scholarly
instead of bubbly and carefree
or dramatic and vivacious
rather than sensible and
serious. Whatever the contrast,
no friendship could ever be as
compelling as the one you have
with your sister.

FOREVER FRIENDS

*Y*ou can take your sister's friendship for granted. It's okay because she takes yours for granted, too. Both of you cherish your relationship all the more because it doesn't need tending.

FOREVER FRIENDS

SISTERS

FOREVER FRIENDS

68

*M*om always said it
didn't take much to entertain
you girls, and it's still true.
Whether you're combing a
dusty shop for just the right
vintage tea cup or up to your
elbows in dirt planting tulip
bulbs, you're having fun,
for the most part, because
you're together.

FOREVER FRIENDS

To say a friend is
"like a sister" is to pay the
ultimate compliment.

FOREVER FRIENDS

SISTERS

Original inspirations by Barbara Briggs Morrow.

PHOTO CREDITS